THE ABC$ OF FINANCE © Copyright 2021
Text copyright © Britt Rozenblat
Illustration copyright © Ayang Cempaka
ISBN: 978-1-77789-31-2-5
Published in Canada, printed in United States of America
Published by The Children's Book Company
All rights reserved.
www.thechildrensbookcompany.com

A is for *ASSET*

Assets are things that hold value to me—like
my piggy bank, cars and the stuffies you see.

B is for *BANK*

A **bank** is a place where my money can go.
My savings will always be safe there, I know.

C is for CREDIT CARD

A **credit card** acts like invisible money.
It buys things like clothes or a small jar of honey.
Remember you *will* have to pay it all back!
So be sure to take notes that will help you keep track

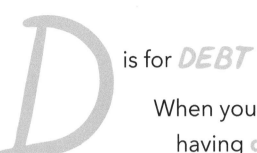

is for *DEBT*

When you owe your friend money, it's called having **debt**. Repay every penny—don't ever forget!

E is for *EARN*

When I help clean my room and put dishes away,
I **earn** an allowance—my cash for the day!

F is for FRAUD

Fraud is like lying—it's not very nice!
Always be honest and very precise.

G is for *GIFT*

Giving a **gift** is a wonderful deed, so try donating toys to some others in need!

H is for **HARVARD BUSINESS SCHOOL**

If **Harvard's** my goal. I'm on the right path:
acing my tests in reading and math.

I is for **INVEST**

Money **invested** will grow into more.
Then you can buy a new building (or four)!

J  is for *JOINT*

Francesca started a lemonade stand.
After a while, Henry lent a hand.
Now they are partners: their business is **joint**.
Working together, they won't disappoint!

K is for **KNOWLEDGE**

The more that you learn, the more you will know.
Knowledge is power that helps your brain grow.

L is for **LOAN**

Olivia loves to share and play.
　　She's letting you use her new toy for the day!

But when the day's over, you must give it back.
　　She **loaned** you her toy and gave you a snack.

M is for *MONEY*

My parents use **money** like dollars to pay ...

for this family vacation here in Saint-Tropez!

N is for *NEGOTIATE*

Crying and stomping, Benny wouldn't share. He wanted one more pretzel and he didn't really care!

Sarah stepped in; **negotiations** began.
She gave him one half—what a perfect plan!

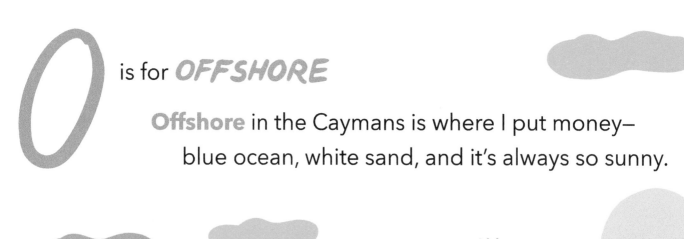

O is for *OFFSHORE*

Offshore in the Caymans is where I put money—
blue ocean, white sand, and it's always so sunny.

BANK

P is for PRICE

Ralph's frozen yogurt is with the cashier. She tells him,

"The **price** is five dollars, my dear!"

Q is for *QUANTITY*

Quantity means just how many there are.

See, here I've got three hundred stamps and one car

R is for *REAL ESTATE*

Real estate includes buildings and land,
like a house in the hills or a tent on the sand.

S

is for **SAVE**

My piggy loves **savings**—she says, "Oink, don't stop!"
The thing she loves most is to hear the change drop.

OINK!

OINK!

T is for TAX

When mum takes me shopping and pays for a bow,

RECEIPT
BOW $5.99
+ TAX
TOTAL $6.58

U is for *UNEMPLOYMENT*

When business is tough, someone could lose their job.
That's called **unemployment**—just ask uncle Rob!

V is for **VALUE**

Some things are worth more every year that goes by.
Like the **value** of gold—it might reach to the sky!

W is for *WALL STREET*

There are so many buildings to see on **Wall Street**. Look—there's Mommy's office and clients she'll meet!

X is for X

We solve some equations in class to find X.
These math-problem mysteries can be so complex!

 is for **YO-YO**

Like a **yo-yo** the stock market goes up and down.
When it gets too expensive it's hard not to frown!

CANDY

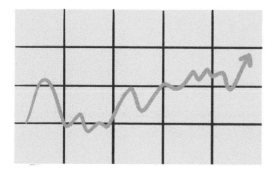

TOYS

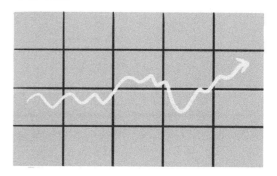

CHIPS

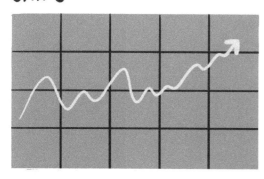

ICE CREAM

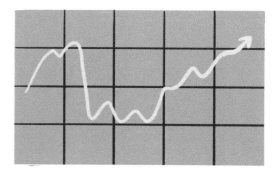

Z is for **ZERO**

I count all the numbers from ten until one.

When I get to **zero**, that means there is none.

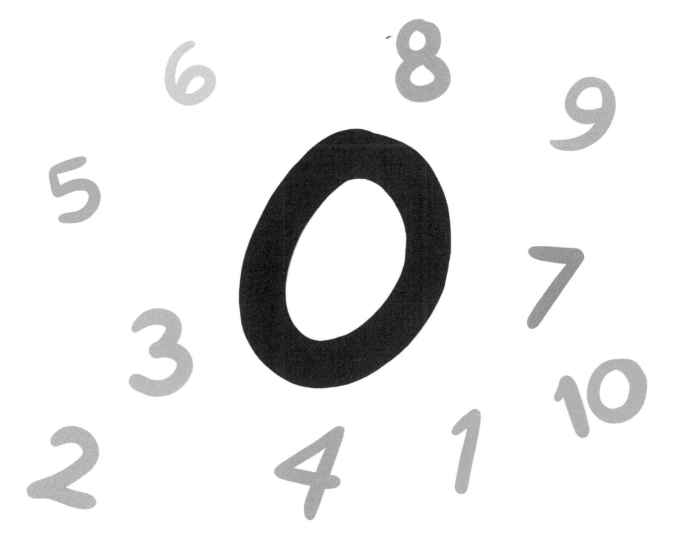

Printed in the USA
CPSIA information can be obtained
at www.ICGtesting.com
LVHW061947120923
757620LV00045B/20